First published in Great Britain by Heinemann Library
Halley Court, Jordan Hill, Oxford OX2 8EJ
a division of Reed Educational & Professional Publishing Ltd

OXFORD FLORENCE PRAGUE MADRID ATHENS
MELBOURNE AUCKLAND KUALA LUMPUR SINGAPORE TOKYO
IBADAN NAIROBI KAMPALA JOHANNESBURG GABORONE
PORTSMOUTH NH CHICAGO MEXICO CITY SÃO PAULO

First edition © Éditions Mango 1995

This edition © Reed Educational and Professional Publishing Ltd 1997

Designed by Marion de Rouvray and Celia Floyd
Illustrations by Sophie de Seynes
Printed in France

01 00 99 98 97
10 9 8 7 6 5 4 3 2 1
ISBN 0 431 05437 1

British Library Cataloguing in Publication Data

Royer, Alain
 The ascension. – (Bible stories)
 1. Bible stories, English – Juvenile literature
 I. Title II. Carpentier, Georges
 221.9 ' 505

Acknowledgements
Our thanks to Jan Thompson and Clare Boast for their comments in the preparation of this book.

Every effort has been made to contact copyright holders of any material reproduced in this
book. Any omissions will be rectified in subsequent printings if notice is given to the Publisher.

BIBLE STORIES

The Ascension

Written by

Alain Royer and Georges Carpentier

Illustrated by

Sophie de Seynes

Heinemann

A few days after Jesus's death, Peter said to Thomas, John and three other disciples, 'I'm going fishing.'

'We'll come with you,' they said.

So Peter and his friends left their house. They got into their boat and went out to sea just as the sun was going down. They fished all night but they caught nothing.

In the morning, Jesus was on the shore. Peter and his friends did not know him at first. Jesus called out to them, 'Friends, have you caught any fish?'

'No!' they said.

'Well, throw your nets over the right-hand side of the boat,' said Jesus.

The disciples did as Jesus told them. They caught so many fish that they could not pull in their nets.

Then John said to Peter, 'It's the Lord!' Peter
dived into the sea and swam to the shore. The
others brought the boat in.

When Peter got closer to Jesus, he saw that Jesus was sitting by a glowing fire. He was cooking bread and fish. 'Bring me some of your fish,' Jesus said to Peter.

Peter went back to the boat that the other disciples were bringing in to the shore. He helped them to pull in the nets. Together they were able to pull the nets in without tearing them.

Jesus asked the disciples to eat with him. He gave them the bread and the fish he had cooked.

After they had eaten, Jesus asked Peter three times, 'Do you love me?' And three times Peter said, 'Lord, you know that I love you.' Then Jesus said to him, 'Be the shepherd of all those who believe in me.'

Some time later, Jesus brought his disciples together. He raised his hands and blessed them. As he was blessing them, a cloud hid him from their eyes. He was taken up into the sky.

While the disciples were staring up into the sky, two men dressed all in white came to them. They said, 'Why are you staring up into the sky? '

The disciples then knew that Jesus had gone to be with his Father, and that he was watching over them. They went back to Jerusalem full of joy.